REVELATION DESCRIBED

BY REV. DAREN DRZYMALA

DEDICATION:

Rev. Timothy Haberly, pastor at Symphony Bible
Church in Buffalo, NY

Rick Tober, my financial advisor and brother
in the LORD

Rev. Ronnie Freeman, a mentor and founding pastor
of Good News Baptist Church in Lynchburg, VA

Rev. Tom Willis and his wife, Joann Willis, who minister to TR Seniors at Thomas Road Baptist Church
in Lynchburg, VA, and all the seniors involved.

To everyone who gave time or finances to help make
this book possible. The LORD knows who you are.
And you are much appreciated.

TABLE OF CONTENTS

Dedication: v

Introduction ix

1. The Revelation of Jesus Christ 17

2. The Seven Churches Represented 25

3. The Throne Room of Heaven 33

4. The Book of Judgment is Opened 39

5. The 144,000 Preacher Boys. 43

6. The Judgments of the Seventh Seal. 47

7. It's Gonna Get A Lot Worse 51

8. The Two Witnesses of the Lord. 55

9. The Key Characters in Revelation 59

10. What's To Come in the Final Drama. 63

11. The Last Seven Devastating Judgments 65

12. The Total Destruction of Mystery Babylon. . 67

13. The Battle of Battles 71

14. The Glorious Millenial Kingdom 75

15. Our New Home 79

16. Three Final Statements 83

INTRODUCTION

Y ou might have heard people, or have seen people holding signs, saying the end is near. Many people say that the end of the world is coming. Well, that is true to a point. The end of the world isn't coming, but the end of the church age is, and Jesus Christ is coming back very soon. In this book, we want to take an overview of the book of Revelation and what it is saying to us today. This book has been overlooked by many preachers and churches, who either feel it is just too hard to understand or it isn't important enough to preach on. This book will not be an exhaustive study on the book of Revelation but rather a simplistic overview in which I will describe the different events. My prayer is that you will receive basic gems from the book and study deeper in Revelation. Also, if you are not saved and Revelation seems to scare you, the time is at hand to give your life to Jesus Christ by trusting in His death, burial, and resurrection, and turning from your sin by repenting, and giving your life to Jesus Christ.

There are many signs that point to the imminent return of Jesus Christ, and His return will be pretribulational. The signs are set before us in the word of God. I would like to share some scriptures. In 2 Timothy 3:1-5, "This know also, that in the last days perilous times shall come. For men shall be lovers of their own selves, covetous, boasters, proud, blasphemers, disobedient to parents, unthankful, unholy. Without natural affection, truce breakers, false accusers, incontinent, fierce, despisers of those that are good, traitors, heady, high-minded, lovers of pleasure more than lovers of God; Having a form of godliness, but denying the power thereof: from such turn away." A lot is said in this passage, but "This know" basically tells us we can know when we are in the last days. I believe we are a minute to midnight on the prophetic clock, and Jesus Christ can return at anytime to call away His church. It says there will be blasphemers; look at how many people today mock, attack, laugh, and deny the truth of Christ and the Bible. It states "lovers of their own selves;" people care today about just themselves and couldn't care less about others. Without natural affection, which is homosexuality, this immoral lifestyle is more prominent now than ever before and slaps God in the face because the bible teaches man and women are to be joined together, not same sex. It also states unholy; we live in a wicked world where the holiness of God is attacked and the lifestyles of individuals goes against the word of God. Just look at the killing by abortion, homosexuality, pornography, drugs, alcohol, rape, child molestations, and on and on. Let us look at 1 Timothy 4:1: "Now the Spirit speaketh expressly, that in the latter times some shall depart from the faith, giving heed to seducing spirits, and doctrines of devils." Before Christ returns, there will be a strong religious spirit over the world that goes against the Bible. Just look at the ecumenical movement and the so called "inter-faith." They say it doesn't matter who you worship and all roads lead to heaven—that is a lie from hell. We see the cults that are daily trying to convert people to their ways. We see the many world religions—such as Islam, Buddhism, and the thousands of other religions—that are Christless and lead to hell. There is but one way, and that is through Jesus Christ. It also states "doctrines of devils." Look at all the so-called churches that deny the fundamentals of the Christian faith like the virgin birth of Christ; sacrifice of Christ on the cross; the bodily resurrection of Jesus Christ; the soon return of Christ; and salvation by grace through faith, not of works, the bible says, lest any man should boast (Eph 2:8-9). Religion is man's attempt to get to God; Christianity is God reaching down to man. In 2 Peter 3:3-4, we read, "Knowing this first, that there shall come in the last days scoffers, walking after their own lusts, and saying, Where is the promise of his coming? For since the fathers fell asleep, all things continue as they were from the beginning of the creation." People will scoff and question us about the coming of Christ, "Where is he?" they will say, but I promise you, Jesus will come again. John 14:1-3: "Let not your heart be troubled: ye believe in God, believe also in me. In my father's house are many mansions: if it were not so, I would have told you. I go to prepare a place for you. And if I go and prepare a place for you, I will COME AGAIN, and receive you unto myself; that where I am, there ye may be also." Jesus Christ promised that He will come again. Right now He is preparing our heavenly home, and very soon He shall come in clouds of glory.

We see the signs of the times in the last days, before Jesus comes back to rapture His church to heaven. There is a problem in the evangelical community, and that problem questions the timing of Christ's return. This author holds to the imminent and pre-trib rapture of the church. Sorry to say, there are other views out there. Some hold to the mid-trib rapture, that the church will go through half of the tribulation before the "great tribulation," which is the second half of the seven years. Others hold to the post-trib rapture, that we will be raptured and come back the same moment; basically, we will go through the whole tribulation period. Some hold to the "ushering in the kingdom" theology, which basically believes things will get better and better until we enter the millennium kingdom. Still there are those who believe in the partial rapture theory, that only "Faithful Christians" will get raptured and others will go through the tribulation. The problem with this view is that in 1 Corinthians 15 it tells we ALL shall be changed in a moment, in the twinkling of an eye. Yet worst of all, there is a theology out there called "preterism," which doesn't believe that

Revelation is prophetic but that all was completed before 70 AD and the fall of Jerusalem.

I would like to look at some scriptures to help us through our study of Revelation that point to the pre-trib rapture. 1 Thessalonians 1:10 says, "And to wait for his Son from heaven, whom He raised from the dead, even Jesus, which delivered us from the WRATH TO COME." Keep in mind the word *wrath* for now. 1 Thessalonians 5:9: "For God hath not appointed us to wrath, but to obtain salvation by our Lord Jesus Christ. Revelation 3:10 reads, "Because thou hast kept the word of my patience, I also will keep thee from the hour of temptation, which shall come upon all the world, to try them that dwell upon the earth." God will keep us from this seven-year period, which will affect the whole world. We must understand God's plan. He worked with Israel, and then at the start of the church age, He is working with the church, believers who have trusted Christ, both Jews and gentiles. Now there is a theology out there called replacement theology, which states Israel failed, so God used the church. This is false. The church is God's plan until the rapture, then He will be working again with Israel in the main picture; this is called dispensational theology. As I stated about being saved from the wrath to come, as Revelation 3 puts it, "the hour of temptation upon the whole world." The word *wrath* is mentioned ten times in Revelation and they all refer to the tribulation period. Titus 2:13:" Looking for that blessed hope, and glorious appearing of the great God and our Savior Jesus Christ." It is called a blessed hope or a happy time. what happiness would there be if we were to go through the tribulation period? That would not be a happy time, but a sad time of despair and hopelessness. Luke 21:36 says, "Watch ye therefore, and pray always, that ye may be accounted worthy to escape all these things that shall come to pass, and to stand before the Son of man." We will escape this seven-year hour that will come upon the whole world. 1 Thessalonians 4:13-18: "But I would not have you to be ignorant, brethren, concerning them which are asleep, that ye sorrow not, even as others which have no hope. For if we believe that Jesus died and rose again, even so them also which sleep in Jesus will God bring with him. For this we say unto you by the word of the Lord, that we which are alive and remain unto the coming of the Lord shall not prevent them which are asleep. For the Lord himself shall descend from heaven with a shout, with the voice of the archangel, and with the trump of God: and the dead in Christ shall rise first: Then we which are alive and remain shall be caught up together with them in the clouds, to meet the Lord in the air: and so shall we ever be with the Lord. Wherefore comfort one another with these words." Not only is this a clear description of the rapture of the church and also a promise of His coming to rapture the church, but look at the last verse; it says to comfort one another. What comfort would there be if we were going through the tribulation period? There would be none. It would probably state, "Prepare now for the worst you will go through," but no, it says to comfort. I take comfort that Jesus is coming back soon, and before the tribulation hour. The last scripture I would like to look at is from the Old Testament, found in Isaiah 26:19-21: "Thy dead men shall live, together with my dead body shall they arise. Awake and sing, ye that dwell in dust: for thy dew is as the dew of herbs, and the earth shall cast out the dead. Come my people, enter thou into thy chambers, and shut thy doors about thee: hide thyself as it were for a little moment, until the indignation be overpast. For, behold the LORD cometh out of his place to punish the inhabitants of the earth for their iniquity: the earth also shall disclose her blood, and shall no more cover her slain." I believe this is an Old Testament prophecy of the coming of Jesus Christ in the rapture and its timing until the indignation is past, which is the tribulation hour.

Now that we have established the signs of the times, the clear scriptures that Jesus is coming back, and that it will be soon, and before the tribulation hour. Now it is time to take our look at the events to follow once Jesus Christ comes back.

CHAPTER ONE

THE REVELATION OF JESUS CHRIST

❧

J esus Christ is given a clear revelation from God to pass onto his servant John, about things that must come to pass. In Revelation the focus is about Jesus Christ. Jesus Christ is the central theme of all the Bible books and is the same central figure here in Revelation. The same must be said for our lives, that Jesus Christ is the most important person in our lives, our actions, our communication and our message. The plan of Christ is revealed in Revelation 1:1-2: "The Revelation of Jesus Christ, which God gave unto him, to shew unto his servants things which must shortly come to pass; and he sent and signified it by his angel unto his servant John: Who bare record of the word of God, and of all the testimony of Jesus Christ, and of all things that he saw." Here we clearly see that Revelation is God's plan to show

Christ, and to reveal it to John who was banished on the island of Patmos for the crime of preaching Jesus Christ. Can you even comprehend what it would be like to be alone on a deserted island for the cause of Christ? Today we have Christians that are ashamed to pray at dinner or share their testimony to a lost person. Here we see God's man dedicated to Christ, and his message didn't quit or give in because he would be cast on a deserted island. Scripture here says that He would show him things that must come to pass. This is a prophetic statement, and all that is listed from Revelation 4 on will occur in the very near future. Like we stated earlier, there are those in the Christian community who believe in a theology called preterism, which believes that everything in the book of Revelation already came to pass by the fall of Jerusalem in 70 AD. Here John will vividly see all things that will happen in the future and describes it in a very literal way. Get ready Church: Christ is coming soon, and then all hell will break loose on the earth.

The blessings of Christ is mentioned in Revelation 1:3: "Blessed is he that readeth, and they that hear the words of this prophecy, and keep those things which are written therein: for the time is at hand." In this passage, we see a threefold blessing for the book of Revelation. Blessed is the person who reads it: there are many people and many churches that avoid Revelation because they say it is too hard, or not important, or that there are many views that no one really knows what to believe. The word of God is clear—read it, read it, read it! And there is also an application for the whole word of God. We need to read it and study so we will know how to give an answer to those who are searching for truth. Not only are we to read it, but also to hear it. We can read God's word, but are we listening or spiritually hearing what the LORD is saying in these last days? Again, too many Christians listen to the word of God and let it go in one ear and out the other. We need to read, hear, and finally, keep it. There is a need to keep and obey the word of God. When we see the seven churches in the next chapter, we need to read about them, listen to how they reacted to the LORD Jesus Christ and His word, and what they did with it. Then the scripture says the time is at hand — get ready, Jesus is coming soon; there is nothing holding Him back from coming, Christ could come at any moment; the question is, Are you ready? Are you saved? If not, give your life to Christ today.

The work of Christ is mentioned in Revelation 1:5-6: "And from Jesus Christ, who is the faithful witness, and the first begotten of the dead, and prince of the kings of the earth. Unto him that loved us, and washed us from our sins in his own blood. And hath made us kings and priests unto God and his father; to him be glory and dominion for ever and ever, Amen" Three statements regarding the work of Christ on His church: First, He loved us. What an awesome statement! Jesus loves you. Too many preachers, preach only condemnation. Now don't get me wrong; we as preachers need to preach against sin and proclaim the justice of God. The clear simple message is that Jesus loves you and gave His life for you on Calvary's cross and was beaten because He loved you. What great love is this that God would send His son to die on an old rugged cross for a lost and wicked world. Not only does He love us and died for us, but the important part is next He washed us from our sins in His own blood. I believe in a bloody theology. There is power in the blood of the LORD Jesus Christ. 1 John 1:9: "If we confess our sins, he is faithful and just to forgive us our sins, and to cleanse us from all unrighteousness." The blood of Christ is the only liquid that can wash away our sins. Satan hates the name of Christ, and the blood of Christ, because at that name every knee will bow, and every tongue will confess that Jesus Christ is LORD. And through the literal blood of the of the LORD Jesus Christ, any sin that you have committed will be cleansed, past, present, and future . We are told in this passage that we are made kings and priests, that we are made priest believers in Jesus Christ after our great high priest, Jesus Christ. And to God be glory for ever and ever. The LORD will always get the glory whether we let Him or not. He deserves it, and all praise and glory is rightfully His.

The promise of Christ is revealed in Revelation 1:7: "Behold, he cometh with clouds; and every eye shall see him, and they also which pierced him: and all kindreds of the earth shall wail because of Him. Even so, Amen." Here we see the promise of Christ to return, but let's clarify something. This isn't the rapture; we will see the rapture in chapter 4 of Revelation. The church is gone until chapter 19. There are two parts to the second coming of

Christ: The first is Christ coming for the church in a twinkling of an eye in chapter 4; and in chapter 19, Christ coming back with the church and every eye shall behold Him. There is a big difference in the two events. It states that every eye shall see him. I believe that those in heaven and hell, and on earth, will see the LORD come back with his church. When Christ first came in Bethlehem, He came as a baby born to serve, and to die for mankind. In the rapture, He will come and call home His church, made up all born again believers, and when He comes back in Revelation 19 He comes back as King of Kings and LORD of LORDS with judgment before Him. It even states those who crucified Him will wail. I believe they will then see the one they killed was indeed who He claimed to be, the messiah who was predicted to be born, crucified and resurrected all the way back in the old testament."

The eternity and deity of Christ is declared in Revelation 1:8, "I am Alpha and Omega, the beginning and the ending, saith the Lord, which is, and which was, and which is to come, the Almighty." Christ wasn't just born into existence at Bethlehem but always existed, even before time as we know it. The Bible tells us in Colossians 1:16a, "For by him were all things created." Jesus Created the world with God the Father and God the Holy Spirit. Not only is Christ the first, but He will be the last. He is eternal, no beginning, and no ending. We as a church will spend all eternity in heaven with Jesus Christ. Again, you see the statement in the passage "which is to come." Very clearly in Revelation, one, we see that Jesus is coming back for his church, and again, with his church. The Almighty: here we see the deity of Christ Jesus is called the Almighty, a name only given to God the Father. But Christ calls Himself the Almighty, and there takes on the claim of deity. Jesus Christ is fully God and fully man and will exist for all eternity.

The revelation from Christ in Revelation 1:9-11: "I John, who also am your brother, and companion in tribulation, and in the kingdom and patience of Jesus Christ, was in the isle that is called Patmos, for the word of God, and for the testimony of Jesus Christ. I was in the Spirit on the Lord's day, and heard behind me a great voice, as of a trumpet, Saying, I am the Alpha and Omega, the first and the last: and what thou seest, write in a book, and send it unto the seven churches which are in Asia; unto Ephesus, and unto Smyrna, and unto Pergamos, and unto Thyatira, and unto Sardis, and unto Philadelphia, and unto Laodicea." Here again we see John all alone on the island of Patmos because of he was a faithful preacher of Jesus Christ. I wonder how many preachers today would still preach if they knew if they were caught they would go to prison or be banished to an island all alone. John was in the Spirit; he was worshiping Christ, regardless of where he was or what he was going through; he stayed in the spirit of the LORD and had continual fellowship with the LORD. It was the LORD's day that Christ revealed to him what to write to the seven churches. I believe this refers to Sunday the first day of the week, the day our LORD was risen, and then we as Christians come together in corporate worship to hear God's word preached and to fellowship with fellow believers. Again we see Christ claiming His eternity and deity. He sent the letter to the seven churches, which I will talk about in the next chapter.

The description of Christ is portrayed in Revelation 1:13-15: "And in the midst of the seven candlesticks one like unto the Son of man, clothed with a garment down to the foot, and girt about with paps with a golden girdle. His head and his hairs were white like wool, as white as snow; and his eyes were as a flame of fire; And his feet like unto fine brass, as if they burned in a furnace; and his voice as the sound of many waters." Basically what we see here is a description of Christ as the great high priest, wearing priestly garments. His head and hair were white, representing purity and holiness. His eyes were a flame of fire, and His feet like fine brass burned in a furnace. This represents His holy indignation of sin that He sees upon the earth, and pretty soon, all hell will break loose on the earth, and men will cry and wail yet repent not. This picture also depicts His authority and sovereignty, Christ is in complete control no matter what is happening on the earth, or what mankind is doing. My friend, the judgment of God is coming very soon to planet Earth; will you be here or in heaven? That depends on what you do with the person and work of the LORD Jesus Christ.

The resurrection of Christ preached in Revelation 1:18: "I am he that liveth, and was dead; and, behold, I am alive forevermore, Amen; and have the keys of hell and of death." Jesus preached very clearly that

He was dead and now is alive forevermore. There are those liberal preachers who claim Christ never rose from the dead; either He was beaten and later woke up in a dark tomb, or He rose again in spirit only, not bodily. Some even believe that He is still dead, that His disciples stole His body. If that were true, why would they go right back to Jerusalem and preach His resurrection knowing they could be killed for His cause; and secondly, after his death they were discouraged disciples and doubters. What happened was they encountered the risen Christ and had a renewed passion for the LORD and preached Christ's resurrection right back in Jerusalem. I declare to you Jesus is alive. He defeated death and hell by His resurrection.

Jesus is the one and only way to God, dead, buried, and risen and coming again. Listen closely; the trumpet is about to sound, and the LORD is about to descend. The time is at hand.

CHAPTER TWO

THE SEVEN CHURCHES REPRESENTED

༺ঌ

I n this chapter I would like to look at the seven churches of Revelation chapters 2-3. I would like to give my view on what the churches are like and how it applies today. There are different views on the churches. I believe they were literal churches in Asia; also, some believe they represent different time periods in church history, which is also a good possibility, and both could go hand in hand. The way I want to approach it is to look at the churches and how scripture identifies them and how we see these churches even today in our world.

The first church that John wrote the letter to on the isle of Patmos was the church of EPHESUS, found in Revelation 2:1-7. I call this church the "backslidden church." This was a church that started out with a deep love for Jesus Christ and His word. As time went on they became cold; in other words, as the passage describes it, they left their first love. Remember when you were first saved, how on fire you were for Christ, you wanted to tell everyone about him. You also wanted to get involved in every ministry in the church. That is how the church of Ephesus was, but as time went on their dedicated service became just an action and they left their first love. They became callous, started to lose their fire and dedication, and became a backslidden church. We see churches like that today, where the fire has left, the power of preaching is gone, the singing of the saints has become the silence of the saints. Many people today say to me, well, I am a Christian but a backslidden Christian. My friend there is no such thing as a backslidden Christian, but there are Christians who are backslidden, and they need to rekindle that fire and love and service for Jesus Christ. They need to return to their first love. I am so glad that God is there when I lose my fire, and I can repent of falling astray, turn back to His power in my life, and once again have a deep committed love for Jesus Christ. Maybe in your life today you have lost that fire. Just go to Jesus, tell Him you're sorry, repent of your ways, ask Him for that Holy Spirit power to fill you again, and to use you like He did in times past.

The next church is called SMYRNA, found in Revelation 2:8-11. I call this church the "persecuted church." Scripture states that they were a poor church but also a church that Christians would be persecuted for their faith. Today, we here say we are persecuted if someone calls us a "holy roller" or laughs at us for our faith in Christ. We know nothing about true persecution. There are millions of Christians around the world who are truly persecuted for the cause of Christ. As the scripture states in this passage, they were persecuted, put in prison, and put to death for simply having faith in Jesus Christ. Christians were fed to the lions, had eyes plucked out, stoned, beaten, imprisoned, and even tortured and killed for their faith. Today, the same thing is going on around the world. Look at what is happening to Christians in Muslim countries being killed for their faith. We need to pray for the persecuted Christians around the world and ask God to help them, guide them, and protect them. The truth is they are praying for us to be more on fire like they are for Christ. What would you do if someone said you would be beaten and thrown into prison and maybe even killed if you didn't renounce your faith in Jesus Christ? Are you willing to stand when no one else is? The old gospel hymn " I have decided to follow Jesus" says, "tho no one join me still I will follow." We sing it in our churches with power, but do we really mean it in our hearts? I pray today that you and I will follow Jesus Christ no matter what.

There is the church of PERGAMOS, which I call the "worldly church." This was a church that wanted Christ and the world together. We can't mix our faith with worldly living. There is too much compromise in this church. We praise the LORD on one hand and dance with the devil on the other. I have heard of terms such as cussing Christians, those who have no problem swearing; or also sipping saints, Christians who have no problem with drinking alcohol; or another as the HBO Christian, which I call the hell-bound box office television. We watch movies that cuss, show nudity, and take the LORD's name in vain, and we have no problem or conviction about it. We sing songs in church about Christ, then listen to music that dishonors Christ and talks about drinking, immorality, adultery, and other ungodly things. We need the church to come back to holiness and biblical separation from the things of the world. Now, we can't become sinless while here on earth, but we can sin less as we follow God's word and read and study it. We can't have it both ways, serve God and the devil at the same time. I challenge you to live a godly life in Christ Jesus, come out from the world, and be separate. In Romans 12:1-2: "I beseech you there-fore, brethren, by the mercies of God, that ye present your bodies a living sacrifice, holy, acceptable to God, which is your reasonable service. And be not conformed to this world: but be ye transformed by the renewing of your mind, that ye may prove what is that good, and acceptable, and perfect will of God." Here Paul states that living holy is reasonable; it should be natural for the believer. Present your bodies, your eyes in what you look at, your ears and what you listen to, your mouth and what you say, and your feet and where you go. This type of life living is Christ-honoring, and in the church, if we follow this, we will not have a Pergamos-type church or a worldly church, but a Christ-honoring fellowship.

There is the church of THYATIRA, which I call the "pagan church." This is a church which has practices and philosophies and traditions that are against biblical Christianity. They are "religious" but not biblical Christians. They have allowed pagan practices to mix with Christianity, and it is truly sneaking in the church today. We have the new age movement, which basically believes you are your own god, no true thing as evil, and their god is themselves in in all creation is a god. This is a dangerous belief system. There are Christians today who preach we are "little Gods." That is a lie from hell—there is one God, and I am just a sinner saved by faith in Jesus Christ. We also see the occult mixing with so-called Christianity, which believes in polytheism, which is the belief that there are many gods out there. This is a clear violation of scripture. The Bible tells us that I am the LORD and there is none else. The ten commandments tell us that we should have no other gods before Him, and also make no graven images. We see certain churches that have graven images and bow down to them. This is idolatry and the worship of an idol, according to God's word. We can also see in the occult holistic health, mind over matter, and other practices, which again go against the Bible and no Christian should be involved in these practices. Also, reincarnation, witchcraft, sorceries, fortune telling, contacting the dead, prayers for the dead, and I could go on and on. But I pray you see my point: This is a pagan church, and there is no Bible involved. I urge you to stay away from this type of church and practices and attend a Bible-believing church, where the Bible alone is preached, and Christ is honored.

Then there is the church of SARDIS, which I call the "dead church." They are religious but dead. I believe this represents many of the modern churches today. They preach a social gospel, not a biblical gospel. They are liberal in theology. They don't hold that the Bible is totally God's word from cover to cover. They preach doing good, not getting saved. This is a spiritually dead church that needs to hear the old fashioned gospel message of Christ.

Next, I want to switch the last two churches around from their order. Here we see the church of LAODICEA. I call this the "apostate church." This is the church that has totally departed from the true faith. They attack all the true biblical fundamentals of the faith. They basically mix paganism, atheism, and multi-faiths together. It really doesn't matter what you believe as long as you believe in something. It is more a social club than a church. I believe when it comes to church representing a time period, we are living in the Laodicean church period. Many of the churches have departed from true biblical Christianity, to a believe-what-you-want religion. If you belong to a church like this, get out fast, for your soul's sake.

The last church I would like to mention is the church of PHILADELPHIA. I call this the "faithful church." This church is true to the bible and believes it from cover to cover. It preaches salvation through Jesus Christ only. It practices holy living. This church is also faithful in evangelism, which is telling people about salvation through Jesus Christ. Proverbs 11:30: "He that winneth souls is wise." The greatest honor is to be able to lead a person to Christ. I remember back in my college days at Liberty University going out and leading people to the saving knowledge of Jesus Christ. This is the type of church you want to attend, and also serve in.

I exhort you to check out the church your involved in and compare with the churches of Revelation, and see if your church is a bible-based, born-again, fundamental church. If not, leave where you are and find one. It will do you an eternity of good.

CHAPTER THREE:

THE THRONE ROOM OF HEAVEN

༄

I n this chapter, we are going to look at Revelation chapters 4-5. Let's start by looking at 4:1, "After this I looked, and behold, a door was opened in heaven: and the first voice which I heard was as it were of a trumpet talking with me; which said, Come up hither, and I will shew thee things which must be hereafter." John was transported to the throne room of heaven to see what was going to happen hereafter. The question arises, "What happens hereafter?" Like most conservative preachers, I believe that what we are reading in Revelation 4:1 is a picture of the rapture. Again, I would like to emphasize the rapture is before the seven year tribulation period, and after the rapture John was able to see, by the power of the Holy Spirit ,things that would occur after the rapture. The church is now in heaven awaiting the seven years until they come back with Christ to Earth to establish the millennial kingdom.

In 4:2-3: "And immediately I was in the spirit: and, behold, a throne was set in heaven, and one sat on the throne. And he that sat was to look upon like a jasper and a sardine stone: and there was a rainbow round about the throne, in sight like unto an emerald." Here we see the glorious description of the LORD and his throne. I can only imagine the beauty of the throne room of heaven and glorious appearance of my God. One cannot totally comprehend the beauty of this description, but the LORD and his throne room beheld all beauty and glory and majesty and holiness and splendor that one could ever see. We also see a rainbow, which depicts God's everlasting covenant with man. What a day that will be when the church is gathered round this glorious throne to behold the beauty of it all.

Revelation 4:4: "And round about the throne were four and twenty seats: and upon the seats I saw four and twenty elders sitting, clothed in white raiment; and they had on their heads crowns of gold." This is a picture of the Church of Jesus Christ after they are raptured to Heaven. They are wearing white raiments because they have been washed by the blood of Christ and the righteousness of Jesus covers them. Then it states crowns. These are the crowns which will be given to believers at the judgment seat of Christ, which takes place right after the rapture in the throne room of heaven. The judgment seat of Christ is only for believers. It is like a reward ceremony; you will be given crowns based on what you did and how you lived since accepting Christ. Then we will lay those crowns back at the feet of Jesus to show him all honor, praise, glory, and worship . The way we live down here after receiving Jesus as savior will reflect what our judgment day will be like. There are different crowns. One is for those who desire his coming—do you want and anticipate the return of Jesus to take you home? Or do you say, I am not ready, please don't come yet? Then there is a crown for faithful preachers, who are committed to the word of God. Preacher hear me clearly: Rightly divide the word of truth like it states in 2 Timothy 2:15. And be faithful in preaching all the word of God, not just what itches ears, like the prosperity preachers or the preachers who focus on experiences. The word of the LORD hits us sometimes right between the eyes and convicts us of sin and causes us to repent and to return to the LORD. There are many preachers out there today who just want a paycheck, and who will tell you what you want to hear. That is a disgrace to the call of the preacher, and he will answer for that.

Revelation 4:8-11: "And the four beasts had each of them six wings about him, and they were full of eyes within: and they rest not day and night, saying, Holy, holy, holy, Lord God Almighty, which was and is and is to come. And when those beasts give glory and honor and thanks to him that sat on the throne, who liveth forever, and ever, The four and twenty elders fall down before him that sat on the throne, and cast their crowns before the throne saying, Thou art worthy, O Lord, to receive glory and honor and power: for thou hast created all things, and for thy pleasure they are and were created." Here we see where the saints of the church age cast down their crowns at the feet of Jesus, but we also see an old fashioned camp meeting worship service. This was the church, and the Seraphim praising and worshiping the LORD Jesus Christ. It states they cried, Holy, holy, holy, which is praise for the Father, the Son, and the Holy Spirit, three in one, a triune God. We can see that these Seraphim are to worship before the throne all the way back in Isaiah6:1-3: "In the year that king Uzziah died I saw also the Lord sitting upon a throne, high and lifted up, and his train filled the temple. Above it stood the Seraphims: each one had six wings; with twain he covered his face, and with twain he covered his feet, and with twain he did fly. And one cried unto another, and said, Holy, holy, holy, is the LORD of hosts: the whole earth is full of his glory." Amazing how the Bible predicted the worship of the seraphim before the throne room of heaven, and here back in Revelation 4 the saints are joining them. What an awesome time this will be when we are in glory worshiping the one who saved us and washed us clean with His precious blood.

Revelation 5:1-4 says, "And I saw in the right hand of him that sat on the throne a book written within and on the backside, sealed with the seven seals. And I saw a strong angel proclaiming with a loud voice, who is worthy to open the book, and to loose the seals thereof? And no man in heaven nor in earth, was able to open the book, neither to look thereon. And I wept much, because no man was found worthy to open and to read the book, neither to look thereon." Here, we see a book in the hands of the one who sat on the throne, our heavenly father, and He held a book in his hands, which contained the seven seals, which were the judgments will come upon the earth. And John cried because no one was able to open the book or look there onto it. He was discouraged, and probably didn't know what to do or what would happen. As we will see, there is only one who can take the book and open it and pour out the judgments of God, and that is the LORD Jesus Christ. Revelation 5:5-7 reads, "And one of the elders saith unto me, weep not: behold, the lion of the tribe of Judah, the root of David, hath prevailed to open the book, and to loose the seven seals thereof. And I beheld, and, lo, in the midst of the throne and of the four beasts, and in the midst of the elders, stood a lamb as it had been slain, having seven horns and seven eyes, which are seven Spirits of God sent forth into all the earth. And he came and took the book out of the right hand of him that sat upon the throne." This lamb that is pictured is the lamb of God who taketh away the sins of the world, none other than the slain, crucified, buried, and risen savior, Jesus Christ. He was the only one who could take the book, and will be able to open it.

Last, in Revelation 5:8-14: "And when he had taken the book, the four beasts and four and twenty elders fell down before the lamb, having every one of them harps, and golden vials full of odours, which are the prayers of the saints. And they sung a new song, saying thou art worthy to take the book, and to open the seals thereof: for thou wast slain, and hast redeemed us to God by thy blood out of every kindred ,and tongue, and people and nations; And hast made us unto our God kings and priests: and we shall reign on the earth. And I beheld, and I heard the voice of many angels round about the throne and the beasts and the elders: and the number of them was ten thousand, and thousands of thousands; Saying with a loud voice, Worthy is the lamb that was slain to receive power, and riches, and wisdom, and strength, and honor, and glory, and blessing. And every creature which is in heaven, and on the earth and under the earth, and such that are in the sea, and all that are in them, heard I saying, Blessing, and honor, and glory, and power, be unto him that sitteth upon the throne, and unto the lamb for ever and ever. And the four beasts said, Amen. And the four and twenty elders fell down and worshiped him that liveth for ever and ever." We see another old fashioned worship service with the church in heaven. The angels and the creatures all worshiped and sang a new song unto the lamb that was slain. I could go on and on here, but the main point is the ultimate worship of the LORD Jesus Christ. We as Christians need to get back to a daily worship of Christ. Worship is not just singing in church but a twenty-four-hour lifestyle. We can experience true peace and joy while here on earth when we truly come into His presence and worship Christ. But one day we will all—and I mean all—sing and shout and worship the lamb that was slain, but lives now forever and ever. AMEN!

CHAPTER FOUR

THE BOOK OF JUDGMENT IS OPENED

In Revelation chapter six, the seven-sealed book is opened. There will be seven seals, seven trumpets, and seven bowl judgments that will occur on the earth. The time is at hand for the wrath of God to be unleased, but even during this judgment upon the earth and God dealing with and using Israel, there is still the gospel call to come to a personal relationship with Jesus Christ. I will now look at the open book and the six seals from Revelation 6:1-17.

Seal one: The antichrist came conquering and to conquer on a white horse. There are some Bible teachers who believe this rider on a white horse is Jesus Christ, but he isn't; he is an imitator of Christ, as we will see later. Jesus will ride on a white horse when He comes back with the church in Revelation 19 for the battle of Armageddon. The scripture says

He comes conquering and to conquer, when Christ comes on a horse He will be called faithful and true, the King of Kings and LORD of LORDS. This false Christ will come to rise in power after the rapture of the church. Just think about millions from the world who will disappear in a second. There will be babies disappearing, coworkers disappearing, pilots disappearing, every kingdom and nation and tribe will see people suddenly disappear. There will be worldwide chaos planes crashing, cars smashing, people screaming, newscasters scrambling, preachers crying, the skeptics denying. The fact is the whole world will be in an uproar wondering what happened. There will be many reasons that people will give. Some might say that a UFO has taken people away. Others might say evolution has reached a high point and people just disappeared. Still others will say that God rid the earth of the wicked. Whatever the news says will be wrong. Jesus has returned, millions disappeared, the world is in chaos, the political spectrum will not know what to do, and on the scene will come this great, charismatic political leader who will calm the people down and claim to be the messiah of that day. Many who didn't believe in Christ when they had the chance will now with open arms accept this false Christ as their hope. I will look more at this antichrist later.

Seal two: There will be a rider on a red horse, which represents worldwide war. Not only is the world going to be in chaos and an uproar, but there will be war like never seen before, nation against nation and kingdom against kingdom. We have seen many wars in the world, but there will be a war unlike any other war that has ever taken place in history, and many people will be killed.

Seal three: There will be a rider on a black horse, which represents worldwide poverty. We think we have it bad now. There are many of places in the world that are poor, yet there are still many places that are financially stable and well-to-do. When this rider comes—and by the way, I believe the riders on the horses are demons after the first horse of the antichrist—this demon will bring worldwide poverty like never seen before. Billions of people starving, not able to pay any bills, totally devastated without any money. This will set the stage for the one world government and currency, which I will talk about later.

Seal four: This rider is on a pale horse, which represents worldwide death, whether it be by sword, war, hunger, and even death by being devoured by wild beasts. Millions of people worldwide will be dying of diseases from sickness and many other causes. This is not a good time for the earth: chaos, wars, poverty, death, and so on. I am so glad that I will not be here during this time, but as I stated earlier, in heaven worshiping the Lamb of God.

Seal five: During this time there will be a cry for justice under the altar in heaven from the saints of God who would be killed in the tribulation period because of their faith in Christ. These are those who rejected Jesus and when the rapture occurred were left behind, and during the tribulation came to saving faith in Jesus Christ, but would have to die for that faith under the authority of the antichrist. Their cry is for God to deal with the ungodly and the world systems and leaders who put them to death. That day will come and God will hear their cry and justice will be done. God's will and way will always be done in His perfect timing.

Seal six: We have seen and heard of earthquakes all over the world, some just minor, others major, but there will be an earthquake like man has never seen before. The sun will become black, and the moon like blood, and during this time the kings of the earth and the mighty men will try to hide themselves. They will even ask for the rocks to fall on them to hide them from Him that sits on the throne. Even knowing this judgment from Him on the throne, they still will not repent and turn to Christ, but curse and blaspheme His holy name.

These are only the first six judgments; there are many more to come. I can't even imagine these six seals and being there when they occurred, or even being forced to die for my faith. I ask you: Do you want to be here or there in glory? As I have said a few times already, give your life to Christ today and be saved from the wrath to come.

CHAPTER 5

THE 144,000 PREACHER BOYS.

❦

In Revelation chapter 7 we see a group of Jewish preacher boys who are sealed with the mark of the Holy Spirit to go throughout the world and preach the gospel of Christ. This is not as the Jehovah's Witnesses believe, that this is the number who will inherit the earth. This is a group of young, fundamentalist preacher boys preaching Jesus with the protection of the LORD. Let's look at Revelation 7:1-4: "And after these things I saw four angels standing on the four corners of the earth, holding the four winds of the earth, that the wind should not blow on the earth, nor on the sea, nor on any tree. And I saw another angel ascending from the east, having the seal of the living God: and he cried with a loud voice to the four angels, to whom it was given to hurt the earth and the sea, Saying, hurt not the earth, neither the sea, nor the trees, till we have sealed the servants of God in their foreheads. And I heard the number of them which were sealed: and there were sealed an hundred and forty and four thousand of all the tribes of the children of Israel." God put a protection upon these preacher boys in their foreheads, just like later the false system of the antichrist will put a mark of man on the foreheads of those who follow his system, and that number is six hundred and sixty six. Once they receive that mark, they are sealed to hell, but this group is protected with the seal of God. In Revelation 7:5-8, it tells us that the preacher boys come from the twelve tribes of Israel, twelve thousand from each tribe.

In Revelation 7:9-17: "After this I beheld, and, lo, a great multitude, which no man could number of all nations, and kindreds, and people, and tongues, stood before the throne, and before the lamb, clothed with white robes, and palms in their hands; And cried with a loud voice saying, salvation to our God which sitteth upon the throne, and unto the lamb. And all the angels stood round about the throne, and about the elders and the four beasts, and fell before the throne on their faces, and worshiped God, Saying, Amen: Blessing, and glory, and wisdom, and thanksgiving, and honour, and power, and might, be unto our God for ever and ever, Amen. And one of the elders answered, saying unto me, What are these that are arrayed in white robes? And whence came they? And I said unto him, Sir, thou knowest. And he said to me, these are them which came out of great tribulation, and have washed their robes, and made them white in the blood of the lamb. Therefore are they before the throne of God, and serve him day and night in his temple: and he that sitteth on the throne shall dwell among them. They shall hunger no more, neither thirst any more; neither shall the sun light on them, nor any heat. For the lamb which is in the midst of the throne shall feed them, and shall lead them unto living fountains of waters: and God shall wipe away all tears from their eyes." This group of murdered saints who were killed for the cause of Christ, will worship the lamb with all the angels, the church in heaven, and the Seraphim and will fall down on their faces and praise the lamb of God. They also will hunger no more, thirst no more, and cry no more. They are home at last, free at last from the evil one. This multitude of murdered saints can now relax and worship the LORD Jesus Christ for all eternity, but for those wicked on the earth, there is more wrath to come.

CHAPTER SIX

THE JUDGMENTS OF THE SEVENTH SEAL

ॐ

The first six seals served as a warning sign to wake people up to turn to the LORD. Now we see the judgments of the seventh seal, which will occur during the second half of the tribulation period or what is known as the great tribulation. Now, we know that Christians go through tribulation periods in their lives, and even great tribulations to them, but that is different from this seven-year tribulation period during which we will now start to see the judgments of the second three and a half years. There is still time for men to turn to God through Jesus Christ. In Revelation chapters 8-9, we will see the six trumpet judgments.

Trumpet one—The Bible describes it as great hail and fire mixed with blood will be *cast* onto the earth, and one-third of the grass and trees destroyed.

All over the over the world, one-third of grass and trees will be wiped out and burned out and will be no more. The judgments are affecting the earth, which will affect the people of the earth.

Trumpet two—A great fireball as a mountain cast into the sea, and a third part of the sea became blood, and a third of the creatures of the sea died, and a third of the ships destroyed. One-third of the world's water supply is now destroyed. I can only imagine what type of effect will take place on the people of the earth.

Trumpet three—A great fiery star called Wormwood, which means bitter, will fall from heaven, and will make one-third part of the earth's rivers, waters, and fountains bitter, and many men will die. The effect is starting to take place; people no longer have clean water to drink but bloody, bitter water, and it causes many men to die. I am so used to going and getting a cold glass of water with no worry, but that won't be the case. The water supply will be extremely dangerous to drink and will cause sickness and disease and finally death.

Trumpet four—A third part of the sun, moon, and stars were darkened, and the day shone for not a third part of it. Now we see a judgment of darkness. We all know when there is pure darkness all the evil happens. The world is now being affected in a mighty way, through the water supply, the lights from the sky, and that is not it; it isn't finished. In Revelation 8:13: "And I beheld, and heard an angel flying through the midst of heaven, saying with a loud voice, Woe, woe, woe, to the inhabiters of the earth by reason of the other voices of the trumpet of the three angels, which are yet to sound." There are three more trumpets to come, and they are worse than the ones before, if that is even possible.

Trumpet five—The fifth trumpet sounded, and here we see the first demonic invasion of demons on the earth for judgment during the great tribulation. They are going to torment people with the deadly sting of a scorpion, and it will not kill them, but they will be tormented in awesome pain for five months. They will cry out to die but will be unable to. I am one who doesn't like pain, but I can't even imagine being attacked by a demon and stung like the sting of a scorpion and not be able to die and crying out in torment day and night. It reminds me a little of what the lake of fire will be like; people who are unsaved in the lake of fire will be in torment day and night for not only five months but all eternity. The time to get saved is today!

Before we look at the next trumpet judgment I want to discuss this issue of demons on the earth. There is a spirit world below. We see this in Ephesians 6:12: "For we wrestle not against flesh and blood, but against principalities, and against powers, against the rulers of the darkness of this world, against spiritual wickedness in high places." The Bible describes a demonic world. We can't see into the spiritual realm, but the demonic world of hell is at work and will manifest in the great tribulation hour. I also believe that we see a demonic invasion now before the rapture in the form of UFOs., Some believe they are from the government, and others beings from other planets.

I believe that they are a last-days' manifestation of demons from hell invading earth. Every story you here about them is not so good. There is no good in the hosts of hell that presently survey the earth; that is just my observation. Now let us look at another invasion of demons upon the earth.

Trumpet six—The sixth trumpet will sound, and there will be two hundred million demons released from hell to kill a third part of men from the earth. Fire will proceed from their mouths and tails like serpents to kill men. And the others who were not killed repented not of their evil ways and turned not to Christ. Some believe that this is an army of men. I believe in the passage in Revelation 9:13-21 that these are indeed demons from hell. The thief comes to kill, steal, and destroy, and that his army from hell sure does in these two invasions of demons upon the earth.

The six trumpets sounded, and there is more to come. People are still being deceived and not turning to Christ.

CHAPTER SEVEN

IT'S GONNA GET
A LOT WORSE

ॐ

Here I will take a short look at chapter 10 of Revelation. I will quote the whole chapter, and make a couple of comments. In this chapter, we see an interlude between the sixth and seventh trumpet. Revelation 10:1-7: "And I saw another mighty angel come down from heaven, clothed with a cloud: and a rainbow was upon his head, and his face was as it were the sun, and his feet as pillars of fire: And he had in his hand a little book open: and he set his right foot upon the sea, and his left foot upon the earth. And cried with a loud voice, as when a lion roareth: and when he had cried, seven thunders uttered their voices. And when the seven thunders had uttered their voices, I was about to write: And I heard a voice from heaven saying to me, seal up those things which the seven thunders uttered, and write them not. And the angel which I saw stand upon the sea and upon the earth lifted up his hand to heaven. And sware by him that liveth forever and ever who created heaven, and the things that therein are, and the earth, and the things that therein are, and the sea, and the things which are therein, that there should be time no longer. But in the days of the voice of the seventh angel, when he shall begin to sound, the mystery of God should be finished, as he hath declared to his servants the prophets." John saw a mighty angel. Some believe this is Christ, but I do not because Jesus nowhere in the bible is called an angel. This is one of God's mighty angels. John was ready to write it down but was told not to. I believe there is a reason that not everything is revealed that could or would happen. There are some things that God just doesn't want us to know. This happens until the seventh angel sounded. I wonder what judgments may occur even before the seventh trumpet.

Revelation 10:8-11: "And the voice which I heard from heaven spake unto me again, and said, go and take the little book which is open in the hand of the angel which standeth upon the sea and upon the earth. And I went unto the angel, and said unto him, Give me the little book. And he said unto me Take eat, and eat it up; and it shall make thy belly bitter, but it shall be in thy mouth as sweet as honey. And I took the little book out of the angel's hand, and ate it up; and it was in my mouth as sweet as honey: and as soon as I had eaten it, my belly was bitter. And he said unto me thou must prophesy again before many peoples, and nations, and tongues, and kings."

I believe that the book he ate tasted good, but the results were bitter, and this represents the judgments to come to all peoples, nations, tribes, and kings. We are still in a period of judgment, but God took a time out before more judgments, the seven bowl judgments, come. The time is surely at hand.

CHAPTER EIGHT:

THE TWO WITNESSES OF THE LORD

૭૭

In Revelation chapter eleven, we see that there will be two witnesses of the LORD who will do signs and wonders and proclaim the message of the LORD. That message has never changed: It is come to faith in Christ by repenting of your sins and believing in the death, burial, and resurrection of Christ. There is much speculation as to who these two witnesses are. I believe that they are Enoch and Elijah, for the reason is that they both never tasted death but in Revelation eleven they will and also see a resurrection.

In Revelation 11:1-6, the scripture tells us that these two witnesses will preach Christ, and Him crucified. They will prophecy and do signs and wonders and cause plagues upon the earth and many miracles. They will preach for three and a half years, and cause a three-and-a-half-year drought upon the earth . If any man tries to harm them or kill them, fire will come out of their mouths and devour their enemies. They are also protected by the Spirit of God for three and a half years.

Revelation 11:7-10 tells us that when the two faithful witnesses have finished their ministry, the beast that came out of the bottomless pit will make war with them. This is the antichrist, and he and his hosts of wicked people will overcome them and kill them. This wicked group believes that they have accomplished a major victory for their leader. The bodies of these two dead witnesses will lay in the streets of Jerusalem for three days and a half. The people will be so excited over their death that they will send gifts to one another like we do at Christmas time. There will be a huge celebration and party going on because the two "Bible fanatics" are now dead. How sad that the people will be so deceived that they will not receive the message but follow the antichrist and rejoice, party, and give gifts when these two men of God are killed. Isn't that like today? People do not want to hear the old fashioned preaching of the bible, but when a minister falls or a Christian messes up they laugh and rejoice. How sad is that? But their party and celebration will not last for long. We shall see again the victory of God, and the power of our LORD.

In Revelation 11:11-12, we see that before the enemies of God's very eyes, the antichrist shall see the real God move in a mighty way. The two witnesses will be raised to dead, I believe, on national television while it is broadcasting live the jubilation of the wicked and the dead bodies of the witnesses in the street. Then they will be raised from the dead and taken up to heaven. Wow! This is awesome. Can you see the faces of the antichrist and his wicked followers? Their faces will drop, and their celebration will turn to crying and discussion to what just occurred. They still will not turn to God, but continue on in their wicked ways and follow their false christ.

In Revelation 11:13, a great earthquake takes place and hits Jerusalem, and a tenth part of the city will fall, and seven thousand men will be killed, and the remnant of God-saved Jews will give God glory. From celebration to devastation occurs; from laughing to mourning; and from watching the dead to becoming dead. They touched God's anointed and look what happened: Judgment fell upon the city where they killed the two witnesses of the LORD.

In Revelation 11:14-19, Jesus is declared with a loud voice ruler and king forever, proclaiming his coming reign, and also heaven prepares for the coming seven bowls. We also see thanksgiving for God's great power over the wicked and the wicked one, and His blessing for the righteousness ones.

I want to ask you a personal question. Are you a witness for the LORD? And are you willing to tell even the most wicked of people about your faith in Jesus Christ? And lastly, are you willing to die for the cause of Christ? We must ponder these questions as we build a strong personal faith to follow Christ even unto death.

CHAPTER NINE

THE KEY CHARACTERS IN REVELATION

༧༠

In this chapter, I will look at key characters of Revelation chapters 12-13, and the role that they play.

The first one is the woman. She represents Israel. God always had a plan and purpose for Israel. We look back in the Old Testament and see the Abrahamic covenant, that God will bless those that bless Israel, and curse them that curse Israel. Israel has always had a special place in the heart of God. Even when they were up and down from worshiping him, to going back to idols, the LORD punished them but still loved them, and kept His promises to them. Israel has always been under attack by most nations of the world, especially the Muslim countries that surround her. She has been under attack, and will in the future be attacked by many leading Muslim nations in the end and will come out victorious.

The second one is the dragon, and the dragon represents Satan, who is presently the "god of this world." He will go about in the tribulation to deceive the whole world to follow the beast and to worship him. But during this tribulation period, many will overcome him by the blood of the lamb and by the word of their testimony. These are called tribulation saints, who will be resurrected and enter the millennial kingdom and reign and rule with Christ and the church and saved Israel.

The third one is the male child. This represents Jesus Christ, who was born from the woman (Israel). This is why Satan hates Israel so much that he does everything in his power throughout history to destroy Israel, even until the end of the millennial kingdom. Satan thought he defeated Christ on the cross, but on the third day, when Jesus rose bodily from the dead, he knew his days were numbered.

The fourth one is the rest of her offspring. This is represented by saved Israel. Satan went to make war with this remnant, which he couldn't stand, but lost because they were covered by the blood of the lamb.

The fifth one is the beast of the sea. This is the antichrist who was able to do great signs and wonders. He was worshiped on earth as the messiah. There comes a point where he will be wounded in the head and die, but Satan will raise him from the dead, just to imitate the resurrection of Christ. But the difference is Christ lives forever and ever, and Satan will one day be cast into the lake of fire.

The sixth one is the beast of the earth. This is the false prophet, a religious leader. Here we have the "unholy trinity:" Satan, the antichrist, and the false prophet, again trying to imitate the triune God. He also did great signs and wonders like the prophets of old. He had an image made of the antichrist, the beast of the sea who was killed and came back to life, and caused the image of the beast to speak. Those who didn't worship the image were to be killed. He also made it a law that all people could not buy or sell anything unless they had the mark of the beast, the number of man on their hands or forehead, which was six hundred and sixty six. Once people took this mark, they sealed their damnation to hell fire, and no repentance or trying to turn back could save them. Yes, they could buy and sell and survive, but their future and destiny was ordained to eternal and spiritual death in the lake of fire, with the devil and his angels. Many of the people who didn't take the mark could not buy or sell, and tried to hide themselves from the antichrist and his world system. If they were caught, they were killed. If they survived the seven years, they would enter into the millennial kingdom.

This whole seven-year period is a devastating time of God's wrath, but also in God's plan to bring Israel to Himself and to judge the lost and wicked and the unholy trinity and the hosts of hell. But great times will soon be coming. Christ will sit on David's throne in Jerusalem, and the saints of old, the church, and the tribulation saints will reign and rule with Christ for one thousand years.

CHAPTER TEN

WHAT'S TO COME IN THE FINAL DRAMA
꿍

I will now talk about Revelation chapters 14-22 and what is yet to come. I will look at some of these in more detail later.

We will see the one hundred and forty four thousand preacher boys again. Some preachers believe this is another group, but I believe they are the same ones we talked about before, they are made up of twelve thousand from the twelve tribes of Israel, and they will be male virgins and virtuous. Some try to spiritualize this and say they really are just kept from the worldly ways. That is true, but I also hold to the literal meaning of virgins — they did not know women in any sexual way. They will preach throughout the tribulation the everlasting gospel of Christ. The message of Jesus has never, nor will it ever, change. Christ was able and willing to save anyone, even during this terrible tribulation hour, who would repent and call upon the name of the LORD.

There will be seven final judgments, called the vials or bowls of God's wrath, that will come. upon the whole world.

The fall of mystery Babylon, which will rise to power and will be destroyed by Almighty God.

The return of Christ, and the battle of Armageddon, where the LORD will receive the ultimate victory.

The millennial kingdom where Christ will be king and rule for a thousand years.

Then I will look at the new home for all the saints of God.

Finally, I will look at three final and awesome statements to conclude the book.

There is still a lot to occur, and until the very end, mankind can still put their faith and trust in Jesus Christ. Have you trusted Jesus yet? If not, do it now and save your soul from hell.

CHAPTER ELEVEN

THE LAST SEVEN DEVASTATING JUDGMENTS

I n this chapter, I will look at the last seven judgments, called the seven vials or seven bowls, found in Revelation chapter 16.

The first bowl judgment is painful sores all over the bodies of those who have the mark and follow the beast. This will be excruciating pain like never before. I have heard from people with all types of sickness and diseases and the pain they go through, and nothing will compare with the open, bloody, and painful sores poured out around the world on the flowers of the beast.

The second bowl judgment will be all oceans and seas polluted, and all ocean and sea life dies, and totally turned to blood. Imagine the smell coming from the ocean and seas, and the blood filled water. Judgment has come and will continue.

The third bowl judgment will be ALL rivers, and fresh fountains of water turned to blood and everything dies. Now the total water supply for the whole world is bad, and there will be nothing to drink. The waters of the world come under God's wrath, and the people will die literally of thirst. I can't even comprehend what it would be like to not be able to have any water and have unquenchable thirst to the point of choking to death.

The fourth bowl judgment will be that the sun's heat intensifies and literally burns men to death. A literal oven of fire upon all flesh who worshiped the beast.. During this judgment, they cursed God's name and didn't repent and didn't give him glory.

The fifth bowl judgment, Darkness, came completely upon the kingdom of the beast, and also an agonizing pain, which is the sores from bowl one. Their pain intensifies, if you can even wonder how, but it does.

The sixth bowl judgment is that the kings of the east cross the dried-up Euphrates river and gather all the kings of the world and their armies to go to get ready for the battle of Armageddon, which is the battle of battles.

The seventh bowl judgment is the world's most fierce and damaging earthquake. Islands fled away, mountains disappeared, nations fell, and great mighty hail from heaven fell upon men, and the great city of the beast was split in three parts. Here yet again, mankind didn't repent or even turn to God, but continued to follow the beast.

CHAPTER TWELVE

THE TOTAL
DESTRUCTION OF
MYSTERY BABYLON

❧

I am going to take a brief look at Revelation 17-18.
In these two chapters, we have many different
views among evangelical Christians. The first one
I would like to address is, Where is this city of
Babylon? This is man's city where the antichrist
rules, but we will shortly see the LORD'S city where
Jesus rules. Many people believe that Babylon is
going to be rebuilt and that will be the headquarters
of the antichrist. Others believe that Babylon will
be America, and still others believe it will be Rome.
Those who believe it will be Rome also believe the
Roman Catholic Church will be heading up the great
harlot, the false religious system of chapter 17. Yet
still some believe it could be any major nation. I per-
sonally believe it will be Rome, which was known

for its paganism and false religious system, and its deep persecution of Christians back then. And in some scriptures like 1 Peter 5:13, which reads, "The church that is at Babylon, elected together with you, saluteth you, and so doth Marcus my son." In this verse, Babylon is a metaphor for Rome, which many believe, and so do I. The Bible also predicts the revived Roman Empire.

So all that said, wherever "Babylon" is, it will have two faces in Revelation 17: the false religious system, which will be the one world religion that will represent the great whore of revelation, and this one world apostate religious system. I believe this will be the ultimate inter-faith, ecumenical system unlike we have ever seen before. In today's society, we have all types of religious gatherings with Catholics, Protestants, and all types of world religions, and usually when they meet, the ones excluded are the Bible-believing Christians who believe the Bible is God's perfect word and Jesus is the only way. Well, in this one world system, I believe it will be made up of Roman Catholics, Apostate Protestants, and all world religions united together to worship the antichrist. Anyone who dares come against them could face death. We are getting closer and closer to this one world government. Every religious view is accepted except for born-again Bible believers. This system will fall by the antichrist when he basically declares himself God and no longer needs the apostate religious system.

Be careful today to get involved with anybody who says we all worship the same God. No we don't;

we worship the God of the Bible, who sets people free through Jesus Christ.

In Revelation 18, we see the fall of the one world government. I quote Rev 18:1-2: "And after these things I saw another angel come down from heaven, having great power; and the earth was lightened with his glory. And he cried mightily with a strong voice, saying, Babylon the great is fallen, is fallen, and is become the habitation of devils, and the hold of every foul spirit, and a cage of every unclean and hateful bird." Also Revelation 18:8: "Therefore shall her plagues come in one day, death, and mourning, and famine; and she shall be utterly burned with fire: for strong is the Lord God who judgeth her." Also Revelation 18:19-21: "And they cast dust on their heads, weeping and wailing, saying, Alas, alas, that great city, wherein were made rich all that had ships in the sea by reason of her costliness! For in one hour she is made desolate. Rejoice over her, thou heaven, and ye holy apostles and prophets, for God hath avenged you on her. And a mighty angel took up a stone like a great millstone, and cast it into the sea, saying, thus with violence shall that great city Babylon be thrown down, and shall be found no more at all." The one world religion is destroyed by the antichrist, and all the governments of the one world government headed by the antichrist in Rome will be destroyed and made desolate by the power of our awesome God.

It doesn't matter how powerful a nation is or how religious a person is; the nation will be brought down by God, and the religious will be sent to hell by God.

The only ones who have true hope are the believers in Christ. The religious and political Babylon is now destroyed, but Satan isn't giving up on defeating Christ, and as we shall see next all the armies of the world try one more time to defeat Jesus Christ.

CHAPTER THIRTEEN

THE BATTLE OF BATTLES

I n chapter 19 of Revelation verses 1-10, there will be the marriage supper of the lamb. This will be a glorious celebration of all who are in Christ. This includes the church, Old Testament saints, and tribulation saints.

But I would like to focus on Revelation 19:11-21. I will go through this great battle, and we see the armies of the world all gathered at Armageddon to try and defeat the LORD. In Revelation 19:11, Christ comes out of heaven on a white horse, and He was called faithful and true. Jesus Christ is indeed faithful to us even when we are not faithful to Him, and He is the true one. There is no other name like Jesus

Revelation 19:12 describes His eyes as a flame of fire. Christ is coming down to show compassion on the lost , but judgment for the wicked

In Revelation 19:13 we see a description of what He is wearing on the white horse. It tells us that He is clothed in a vesture dipped in blood, and His name is called the word of God. A bloody vesture pictures the blood He shed on Calvary's mountain, and His name is the word of God, which Christ is also called in John 1:1.

In Revelation 19:14, there are armies following behind him on white horses, clothed in fine linen, white and clean. This is finally the church that was raptured in Revelation chapter 4:1, and they have white garments because they were washed in the blood of Christ.

In Revelation 19:15, Jesus speaks the word out of his mouth, and the nations were destroyed. The word of God is powerful. It created the world in six literal days, and his word makes demons and Satan tremble. We as Christians are told to proclaim God's word, and preachers, preach it even when it is despised and hated.

In Revelation 19:16, on the vesture of Jesus Christ is written King of Kings and LORD of LORDS. Christ isn't coming as a humbled servant, but a God of justice against sin, and the King of Kings is His name.

In Revelation 19:17-18, God calls all the fowls of the air together for what is called a great supper, but not one that you and I would like to partake of. When the LORD destroys the armies of the world, and the dead flesh lay on the ground, these fowls are going to have a flesh feast. Verse 21 says all the fowls were filled with their flesh.

Revelation 19:20: This is where the false prophet and the beast are cast into the lake of fire, which was prepared for the devil, and his angels. Later, Satan will be sent there, and the unsaved who are presently in hell will be cast into the lake of fire.

I don't want to see anyone go to hell, so if you're reading this and get kind nervous about your own spiritual condition, give your life to Jesus Christ today and you will be free and free indeed.

CHAPTER FOURTEEN

THE GLORIOUS MILLENIAL KINGDOM

༄

I n this brief chapter, I would like to share some thoughts about the thousand-year reign of Christ, after the battle of Armageddon found in Revelation chapter 20. During this time, Jesus Christ will reign and rule in HIS kingdom. Remember Babylon was the kingdom of the antichrist. Well, this is Christ's kingdom, and it is completely different. Satan will be bound for a thousand years during this time, but when it's over will be released for a short period and try to gather nations to defeat Christ one last time, but God will destroy in a heartbeat, and he will be cast into the lake of fire. Let's look at Revelation 20:10: "And the devil that deceived them was cast into the lake of fire and brimstone, where the beast and the false prophet are, and shall be tormented day and night forever, and ever." When it states that in the lake of fire there is torment forever and ever, this means what it says: There is a real burning fire and torture by demons for all eternity. The suffering of the lake of fire will never end for the lost, and heaven's glory will never end for the saved.

During this kingdom period, there will be no more wars, and Jerusalem will finally be at peace. Let's look at Micah 4:3: "And he shall judge among many people, and rebuke strong nations afar off; and they shall beat their swords into plowshares, and their spears into pruning hooks: nation shall not lift up a sword against nation, neither shall they learn war anymore." Today, there are wars all over, and rumors of wars. Wars will continue until the millennial kingdom where there will be peace, joy, and happiness.

There will be peace among animals and with animals. Let's look at Isaiah 11:6-9: "The wolf also shall dwell with the lamb, and the leopard shall lie down with the kid; and the calf and the young lion and the fatling together, and a little child shall lead them. And the cow and the bear shall feed; their young ones shall lie down together: and the lion shall eat straw like the ox. And the sucking child shall play on the whole of the asp, and the weaned child shall put his hand on the cockatrice's den. They shall not hurt or destroy in all my holy mountain: for the earth shall be full of the knowledge of the LORD, as the waters cover the sea." Here we see animals that would fight and eat one another lying down together in peace, and children playing over the whole of asps. What a peaceful description of what it will be like in this kingdom.

Then there will be the great white throne judgment of all the lost of all the ages found in Revelation 20:11-15. "And I saw a great white throne, and him that sat on it, from whose face the earth and the heaven fled away; and there was found no place for them. And I saw the dead, small and great, stand before God; and the books were opened: and another book was opened, which is the book of life: and the dead were judged out of those things which were written in the books, according to their works. And the sea gave up the dead which were in it and death and hell delivered up the dead which were in them: and they were judged every man according to their works. And death and hell were cast into the lake of fire, this is the second death. And whosoever was not found written in the book of life was cast into the lake of fire." Here we see all the lost getting judged and being taken from hell and cast into their eternal destination called the lake of fire. The Bible describes this as the second death. There is an old saying: born once, die twice; born twice, die one. This basically means if you're born again in Jesus Christ, you will never face the second death. This passage talks about the unsaved being judged based on their works. It seems to me that there will be degrees of hell fire for the lost, but whether there is or not really doesn't matter. The lake of fire is an eternal destination forever and ever and ever in torment. For the Christian, there will be a new home forever and ever and ever. Amen!

CHAPTER FIFTEEN

OUR NEW HOME

ও

Finally, we are home as believers, where we will spend eternity forever more. The home we will spend it in was prepared for us by our savior. We read in John 14:2-3, "In my father's house are many mansions: if it were not so, I would have told you. I go to prepare a place for you. And if I go and prepare a place for you, I will come again, and receive you unto myself; that where I am, there ye may be also." Jesus promised He would go to His Father's house and build a place for us, a beautiful city whose maker and builder is God. This we see in Hebrews 11:10: "For he looked for a city which hath foundations, whose builder and maker is God." Also in Hebrews 11:16: "But now they desire a better country, that is, an heavenly: wherefore God is not ashamed to be called their God: for he hath prepared for them a city."

This new home is described in Revelation chapters 21-22. I would like to look at this city and what it is like. It will be like a place we have never, ever seen, or even could imagine. The scripture I quoted above in John 14 states *mansions*. We will have our own mansion. I don't know about you, but I can't even reckon what it would be like to have my own mansion. Where our mansion will be, there will be a new heaven and a new earth; also a new Jerusalem coming down from God out of heaven. Most importantly will be our leader, who will be Jesus Christ the Messiah.

The Bible describes the beautification of the city, and I would like to list some of the beautiful attributes of our new home.

It will be a city built foursquare, and the length is twelve thousand furlongs, which means the city will be fifteen hundred miles in each direction, and in the city foursquare all the saints of God will dwell.

This city will have a wall with twelve gates of heaven three on each side of the walls. There will be names to the gates, and they will be the names of the twelve tribes of Israel, and each gate is made of a large, beautiful pearl. That is why you hear the expression "the pearly gates." The wall will be made of pure jasper, which was the last stone on the breastplate of the high priest. The foundations of the wall were made up of all types of precious and beautiful stones.

The city will be made of pure gold, like unto clear glass, and the streets of the city are also made of gold, and as transparent glass. Wow, what a picture: Gates of pearls, walls of Jasper, foundation of precious stones, the streets of pure gold, and a city like clear glass. The picture here in Revelation just gives us a glimpse of glory. I am sure there is a lot more that the LORD didn't show John.

There will be no more night or darkness, and no sun, moon, and stars, for the light of the city is Jesus Christ. Today, Jesus is the light which shines in a dark, sinful world, pointing people to Himself.

There will be a clear crystal river that proceeds from the very throne of God and the lamb.

Not only is the city beautiful; it will have physical perfection found in Revelation 21:4: "And God shall wipe away all tears from their eyes; and there shall be no more death, neither sorrow, nor crying, neither shall there be any more pain: for the former things are passed away." In our new home, we will not shed a tear for sadness and sorrow shall flee away. There will be no more sadness of losing a loved one or death of a friend. Neither will there be any more pain and suffering. Diseases and sickness will be gone. The blind shall see, the deaf will hear, and the lame will walk again. This type of physical perfection will only be in our new home. Until then we must suffer pain, sorrow, sickness, sadness, and even death. But one day soon the former will be past, and we will live in Glory and physical perfection forever, and ever, amen

In our new beautiful and physically perfected home will also be a home of spiritual perfection. In Revelation 21:27: "And there shall in no wise enter into it anything that defileth, neither whatsoever worketh abomination, or maketh a lie: but they which are written in the lamb's book of life." In our new home, children will be safe from predators, ladies will be safe from rapists, no murders, no witchcraft, no sin whatsoever. You will not have to deal with an evil thought or action.

In our new home we will be in glorified bodies, traveling through the new heaven and new earth, praising the LORD all the time, talking with the saints of old, and never have another physical problem or a sinful battle, but our new home is perfect, and it is our home for all eternity. The sad part now is that as much as we as believers have a future heavenly home, unbelievers have a future home of hell fire. So let's win as many people as we can to Jesus before it is too late.

CHAPTER SIXTEEN

THREE FINAL STATEMENTS

❧

In this last chapter, which will represent the end of Revelation, I would like to look at three final statements in scripture.

The first one is "The final invitation" found in Revelation 22:17: "And the Spirit and the bride say, Come and let him that heareth say, Come. And let him that is athirst come. And whosoever will let him take the water of life freely." The last invitation in scripture is compelling people to trust Jesus Christ as savior. If you are not sure of your salvation, call upon the LORD today, confess your sins, and turn from them, and trust in the death, burial, and resurrection of Jesus Christ, and ask him to come into your life and save you. If you do this with sincerity, you will be a born-again believer. Then I encourage you to start reading your Bible, probably start in the book of John. Find a good Bible-believing, and Bible-preaching church and attend it regularly. Talk to the LORD daily in prayer, and grow in the grace and knowledge of the LORD Jesus Christ.

The second one is "The final indignation" found in Revelation 22:18-19: "For I testify unto every man that heareth the words of the prophecy of this book, if any man shall add unto these things, God shall add unto him the plagues that are written in this book: And if any man shall take away from the words of the book of this prophecy, God shall take away his part out of the book of life, and out of the holy city, and from the things that are written in this book." God warns about adding and subtracting from the word of God. I would like to look at three scriptures that talk about this subject. Deuteronomy 4:2: "Ye shall not add unto the word which I command you, neither shall ye diminish ought from it, that ye may keep the commandments of the LORD your God which I command you." Deuteronomy 12:32: "What thing soever I command you, observe to do it: thou shalt not add thereto, nor diminish from it." And Proverbs 30:5-6: "Every word of God is pure: he is a shield unto them that put their trust in him. Add thou not unto his words, lest he reprove thee, and thou be found a liar." The Bible is clear about adding and taking away from the pure, complete word of God. When one adds or takes away, it causes major errors and false teaching. I would now like to look at three other scriptures that talk about the results of playing games with God's word. 2 Peter 2:1-2: "But there were false prophets also among the people, even as there shall be false teachers among you, who privily shall bring in damnable heresies, even denying the Lord that bought them, and bring upon themselves swift destruction. And many shall follow their pernicious ways, by reason of whom the way of truth shall be evil spoken of." 1 Timothy 4:1: "Now the Spirit speaketh expressly, that in the latter times some shall depart from the faith, giving heed to seducing spirits, and doctrines of devils." And Galatians 1:6-8: "I marvel that ye are so soon removed from him that called you into the grace of Christ unto another gospel: Which is not another; but there be some that trouble you, and would pervert the gospel of Christ. But though we, or an angel from heaven, preach any other gospel unto you than that which we have preached unto you, let him be accursed." The results of adding and taking away from God's word bring false teachers, false doctrines, false gospels, and damnable heresies. We need to stay true to the Bible, not the book of Mormon, nor the Koran, nor even the Apocrypha; and be careful of many of the modern versions of the bible. We need to watch out for Satan's subtleness in twisting God's word, and hold to the sixty-six books of God's word, nothing more and nothing less.

The third one is "The final proclamation" in Revelation 22:20: "He which testifieth these things saith, Surely I come quickly. Amen. Even so, come, Lord Jesus." John proclaimed his desire for Jesus to come. Are you looking for Jesus to come back? Are you anticipating it? And are you ready for it? Ready or not, Jesus Christ is coming back!

I pray this short overview of Revelation has been a blessing to you, and that you want to dig deeper into the book and the Bible itself. Remember, Jesus loves you and wants to save you, so if you haven't already, give your heart to Christ today

CPSIA information can be obtained
at www.ICGtesting.com
Printed in the USA
FFOW04n0443260314
4519FF